GOVERN
the
INNER REPUBLIC

Copyright ©2025 Kris Wilder and Lawrence A. Kane.

This book was written for humans by humans.

All rights reserved. No part of this publication may be reproduced, distributed or transmitted in any form or by any means, including photocopying, recording, or other electronic or mechanical methods, without the prior written permission of the publisher, except in the case of brief quotations embodied in critical reviews and certain other noncommercial uses permitted by copyright law. Any use of this intellectual property for text and data mining or computational analysis including as training material for artificial intelligence systems is strictly prohibited without express written consent. For permission requests, contact the authors via email: Kris Wilder (kriswilder@kriswilder.com) or Lawrence Kane (lakane@ix.netcom.com).

Stickman Publications, Inc.
Seattle, WA 98126

ISBN-13: 979-8-9916023-1-0

Cover design and interior layout by Kami Miller.

Disclaimer: Information in this book is distributed "As Is," without warranty. Nothing in this document constitutes a legal or medical opinion, diagnosis, or treatment regimen, nor should any of its contents be treated as such. Neither the authors nor the publisher shall have any liability with respect to information contained herein. Further, neither the authors nor the publisher have any control over or assume any responsibility for websites or other external resources referenced in this book.

GOVERN *the* INNER REPUBLIC

Mastering the State Within

KRIS WILDER & LAWRENCE A. KANE

Table of Contents

Introduction ix
1. Silence, Strength, and Sovereignty 1
   Cultivating Silence 3
   Training the Body and Mind with Deliberate Intensity 7
   Observe Without Attachment, Act Without Hesitation 11
   Do Not Seek Comfort, Seek Clarity 15
2. Master Your Voice and Shape the World 19
   Speak as an Architect not an Echo 21
   Use Language to Shape Reality not Decorate Confusion ... 25
   Speak Like You Move, Move Like You Speak 29
   Do Not Perform, Construct 33
3. Build Your Life Brick by Brick 35
   Building What Reflects Your Values 37
   Create Systems, Not Slogans 41
   Promote with Boldness, Serve with Depth 45
   Live with Precision and Purpose 47
   Embody the Cause, Do Not Chase the Effects 49
4. Step Back to Level Up 53
   Retreat to Refine, Return with Resolve 55
   Retreat for Many Reasons 59
   Nourish the Soul Before Raising the Voice 65
5. Own Your Truth, Leave Your Mark 69
   Accept Reality, Shape Legacy 71
   Turn Conflict into Opportunity 75
   Understand Systems before Critiquing Them 79
   Move Toward the Good, not Toward the Crowd 83
   Legacy is Fidelity in Quiet Hours 87
Conclusion 93
Profiles of Wisdom 95
About the Authors 109

"The soul is dyed the color of its thoughts. Think only on those things that are in line with your principles and can bear the light of day. The content of your character is your choice. Day by day, what you do is who you become. Your integrity is your destiny; it is the light that guides your way."

———————————————

HERACLITUS

Introduction

> "I HAVE ALWAYS RECKONED THE
> DIGNITY OF THE REPUBLIC OF FIRST
> IMPORTANCE AND PREFERABLE TO LIFE."
>
> — Julius Caesar

The word "republic" comes from the Latin, *res publica*, meaning commonwealth. The power of a republic resides with the people and their elected representatives. Here, we are talking about the mind, the consciousness, the body, and the energy going in and out of our lives. These elements constitute our own personal republic.

You are a republic.

In a world of endless noise, the most radical act is to become internally ordered. "You have power over your mind, not outside events," wrote Marcus Aurelius. That idea remains the cornerstone of personal sovereignty. To govern the inner republic is to become the architect of your own clarity, to be the steward of your own energy and the strategist of your own response. This book is not about withdrawal; it is about command.

Most people live in a state of internal occupation. Thoughts are colonized by headlines. Moods dictated by algorithms, actions shaped by reaction. The inner republic, once meant to be a sanctuary of reason and will, has become a battleground. A battleground of distraction and emotional volatility.

The causes are structural and spiritual. We've outsourced attention to devices. We have outsourced meaning to movements, and outsourced identity to feedback loops. Descartes warned that, "The greatest minds are capable of the greatest vices as well as of the greatest virtues." Without governance, even brilliance becomes chaos. The Desert Fathers saw this centuries ago. They chose solitude not as an escape, but rather as a strategy.

Our reaction to tumultuous times is often fatigue, cynicism, or compulsive engagement. People scroll, argue, retreat, repeat. They feel the erosion but lack the map to navigate to a better place. Miyamoto Musashi would call this, "Being entangled with preferences." Mike Mentzer would call it, "Irrational overtraining."

This problem is solved by reclaiming the throne of the mind. Not through suppression, but through structure. Not through detachment, but through deliberate rhythm. The inner republic thrives when its ruler is awake, trained, and aligned.

It is solved because the architecture of the self is not broken, it is neglected. Like Plato's ideal city, the soul has its guardians, its workers, and its rulers. When the ruler, the rational faculty, takes command then the city flourishes.

Begin each day with a silent audit: What am I thinking? Why? This builds mental sovereignty. This act alone reveals hidden patterns and aligns intention with awareness. The silent audit turns thought from reaction into strategy before the day even begins.

Train the body with intensity and brevity. Let effort be rational. If you are not doing something physical, you are failing your body. Fail your body and fail the very house in which you live. And there is no opportunity to move to another, better place. You're all you've got.

Limit inputs. Curate your sources like philosophers' curate their arguments. What you choose to take into yourself begins to become you. It's a self-fulling prophecy, an inescapable feedback loop much like the Ouroboros that continuously consumes itself.

Speak less. When you do speak, speak with rhythm and precision. Every word becomes a tool, measured, memorable, and aligned with your intent. The alternative is to have your words discarded like a used fast-food wrapper.

Withdraw weekly. Not to escape, but to refine.

Pray, reflect, or meditate, whatever resonates best. In other words, anchor the soul before engaging the world. Those who reject alignment find themselves in a world created by and for their imperfections. This world of self-creation, based on wants, desires, and envy, requires all things better to be destroyed. This destruction feeds the bad we create.

In a native American parable relayed by the Nanticoke Indian Tribe, a Cherokee elder tells his grandson the tale two wolves, representing good and evil, who are in a constant battle inside every person. The malevolent wolf embodies negative emotions like anger, greed and jealousy, while the virtuous wolf represents positive feelings like compassion, joy, and love. When asked which wolf wins, the grandfather replies, "The one you feed."

To govern the inner republic is not a metaphor, it is a mandate. It is the foundation of every outward act, every creative impulse, every civic stance. The world does not need more reaction. It needs more rulers of the self.

Begin here. Begin now.

Your republic awaits.

1. Silence, Strength, and Sovereignty

> "Over himself, over his own body and mind, the individual is sovereign."
>
> — John Stuart Mill

Our first chapter focuses on reclaiming your personal sovereignty through practices that cultivate clarity, discipline, and presence. It emphasizes the importance of silence as a tool for mental refinement. Drawing on wisdom from luminaries as diverse as Marcus Aurelius and Miyamoto Musashi, you will discover actionable insights that align your thoughts, actions, and intentions, fostering mastery and integrity in your daily life. Soon you will find yourself acting with deliberate intensity while training your body and mind, observing life without attachment, and acting decisively as you apply newfound wisdom to navigate your everyday challenges.

Cultivating Silence

"Silence is the sleep that
nourishes wisdom."

— Francis Bacon

Miyamoto Musashi wrote, "Do nothing which is of no use." Silence, when cultivated, becomes one of the most useful disciplines. It's not passive. It's not retreating. It is refinement.

In today's world, silence is rare. Not necessarily because sound is everywhere, but rather because everyone's attention is scattered. The problem isn't noise, it's fragmentation. Most people wake up, turn to their smartphone, and immediately absorb the world's agenda. We follow a program of notifications, headlines, opinions, and distractions. When others set the agenda, our ability to see clearly and choose wisely is dulled by the time the day begins.

The causes are layered. First, we've been conditioned to equate silence with emptiness. In a culture of constant stimulation, silence feels like a void that needs to be filled. In fact, silence is an effective interrogation technique. Second, we've outsourced our thinking to external inputs. Algorithms curate our moods. Trends shape our beliefs. We reflexively consume more than we contemplate.

Drawing on writings from the Greek philosopher Heraclitus, Marcus Aurelius warned, "The soul becomes dyed with the color of its thoughts." If those thoughts are borrowed, scattered, or reactive, the soul loses its hue. Silence is the space where original color returns.

The reaction to this fragmentation is often anxiety, impulsiveness, or fatigue. People feel overwhelmed, yet under-informed. They speak quickly, decide hastily, and regret quietly. We see this played out every day via the Dunning-Kruger effect, a cognitive bias where people with low ability tend to overestimate their skill, whereas highly skilled individuals tend to underestimate their abilities.

Mike Mentzer would call this "irrational effort," energy spent without structure. The Desert Fathers would call it "spiritual clutter." Elon Musk might say, "Too many meetings, not enough thinking."

The solution is not silence for silence's sake. It's cultivated silence, intentional, rhythmic, and structured. When silence is practiced daily, it becomes a forge. Thoughts settle. Patterns emerge. Judgement sharpens.

The great philosopher, scientist, and mathematician René Descartes began his method with doubt, but he required silence to hear his own reasoning. According to the tale, Descartes saw a fly crawling on the ceiling of his room. He began thinking about how to describe the fly's position. This thought led to the idea of using perpendicular lines and numerical coordinates to define location.

This anecdote is often used to illustrate the birth of the Cartesian coordinate system he published in 1637 which is fundamental in fields like engineering, computer science, and cartography today based on its ability to define and analyze positions and relationships with precision. While the story remains unvalidated, it illustrates the power of silence nonetheless.

Musashi trained alone, not to isolate, but to refine. St. Anthony withdrew into the desert, not to escape, but to confront the inner noise. Silence is not the absence of sound. It is the presence of sovereignty. A foundation of your personal republic.

Silence reveals what noise conceals. The designer of discrimination already exists within you; it's buried. When silence is cultivated, the mind stops reacting and starts observing. The body stops rushing and begins to align. The spirit stops grasping and starts anchoring.

Observing, aligning, and anchoring are the direct result of silence.

Silence is not a retreat; it's a return. It's the space where selectivity is sharpened, where rhythm is restored, and where mastery begins. Plato said, "The beginning is the most important part of the work." Follow his admonition and begin with silence. Begin with sovereignty.

Begin again, each and every day.

Cultivate silence.

Training the Body and Mind with Deliberate Intensity

"Without conscious and deliberate effort, inertia always wins."

— Tony Hsieh

Many athletes, businesspeople, creatives, students, and martial artists struggle with a quiet erosion of purpose. Training of the republic becomes routine. The mind drifts, so the body moves but the spirit doesn't follow.

Intensity fades in athletic endeavors not because we lack strength, but because we lose connection. We forget why we began. We forget what it means to be fully alive in the act. This isn't burnout. It's something subtler, a dilution of intention. Here are a few items that can contribute to varying degrees:

In a world of infinite inputs, our attention is fragmented by distraction. We train our craft, whatever it is, while thinking about emails, texts, errands, or outcomes. Discipline becomes a backdrop, not a sanctuary.

Rituals can mark the beginning and end of training such as we find this in classical martial arts. Rituals are not routine. They are chosen, or adopted, but you make the choice. Rituals signal transition. A practice loses its sacred shape when we enter without reverence and exit without reflection. This is one of the reasons why classical martial artists bow to their training equipment before and after use, even though they are addressing inanimate objects.

The body may be engaged, but the mind wanders. We repeat drills without embodying them. Go to work without sensing the deeper rhythm. We chase the moment but forget presence, so we stand apart from it.

Marcus Aurelius wrote, "You could leave life right now. Let that determine what you do and say and think." That's deliberate intensity. That's the antidote to all this distraction.

When we notice this drift, it can feel disheartening. We might question our discipline, our motivation, even our identity. But at this moment, this noticing is special. It means we're awake. We're aware.

The Desert Fathers taught that awareness is the first step toward transformation. They didn't seek perfection, they sought presence. And presence begins with noticing the absence.

Deliberate intensity is not about doing more. It's about being more involved in what you do.

It is solved through ritualized entry to a moment. You likely have rituals that lie unobserved. See them and ask the question, "Does this ritual suit me? Does this repeated pattern help me ascend to where I want to be? Or it is my ritual, landlocked like a county that has no ships?"

Repetition of successful patterns is important. The desire is to master the ritual, to get it right, sure that's important, but don't seek to master the ritual, strive to meet it.

This is how Musashi trained. With clarity. Just days before his death, he wrote in *Dokkodo*, "Do nothing which is of no use." Every contact with another person, every step, every breath can be deliberate.

This is true because the body and mind are not separate. When one is engaged fully, the other follows. If you can control the mind, you can control the body. Conversely, if you can control the body, you can control the mind.

We've all heard of the winner's mindset. It involves a strong desire to be the best, mentally pushing past physical limitations, handling adversity with resilience, and maintaining composure under pressure. In every sport, greatness stems from an unwavering drive to excel bolstered by a belief that mental strength is as critical, if not more so, than physical talent.

These ideas are not a mood. They are a decision.

With this, we reclaim our practice as a living ritual. We stop outsourcing our focus to external motivators. We become the source. This is why monks can sit in silence for hours and emerge radiant. It's not the posture, it's a presence. Deliberate intensity is not reserved for warriors or monks. It's available to anyone willing to show up fully.

In a world that rewards speed and spectacle, this kind of training is revolutionary. It's quiet. It's personal.

It's sacred.

So, whether you're in a mountain cabin or a garage, a gymnasium or a boardroom, remember this, intensity is not force. It's focus.

When you direct your intention physically and you do so with deliberate intensity, you don't just strengthen your body, your mind comes along as well. That will serve you in all walks of life.

You illuminate your path.

Observe Without Attachment, Act Without Hesitation

> "A FEELING OF AVERSION OR ATTACHMENT
> TOWARD SOMETHING IS YOUR CLUE
> THAT THERE'S WORK TO BE DONE."
>
> — RAM DASS

Observe without attachment. Act without hesitation. It's a phrase that sounds simple, but it's forged in fire. It asks us to see clearly, without clinging. To move decisively, without delay. And to live in a way that honors both awareness and action.

Many people from all walks of life struggle with a subtle paralysis. We hesitate. We overthink. We cling to outcomes, identities, or expectations.

Annie Duke, a former professional poker player, calls this, "resulting." Resulting is the common mistake of judging the quality of your choices solely based on the outcome you obtained rather than on the quality of your decision-making process. It is a cognitive bias that can distort learning and personal growth by conflating luck with skill.

In war, this shows up as a delay. In life, it shows up as indecision. We see the opening, but we don't strike. We feel the truth, but we don't speak. The problem isn't a lack of skill. It's a fog of attachment.

Mental clutter can be a culprit in delaying our choices. We carry too many thoughts into any given moment. What if I fail? What will they think? What does this mean?

Our ego is a driver in the decision-making process. We identify with our roles, our reputations, our past victories. We hesitate because we're protecting an image. And as a result of these needs placed on us by our own ego, we look to the group for the way forward, the correct choice. The safe choice. This can manifest as imposter syndrome, a psychological pattern where individuals doubt their accomplishments and have a persistent fear of being exposed as frauds, despite evidence of their competence.

Fear of loss is greater than the possible joy of winning. Humans are built to cling to comfort, certainty, and control. We are hesitant to make a move when the possibility of loss looms large in our minds.

The samurai knew this well. In *Hagakure*, it is written, "The way of the warrior is resolute acceptance of death." That is not morbid, it is liberating. When nothing is clung to, everything becomes clear. Everything is possible.

In a personal example, walking away from his grandfather's grave after his burial, Kris mentioned something about death to his father. The response was, "We all get to do it." It was nothing more than an acknowledgment of the terminal aspect of our lives. Not a lament, or bemoaning, just a simple acceptance of the order of life. We live, we die, there's no alternate ending.

When we notice this hesitation, born of potential loss, it can feel frustrating. We might question our courage, our clarity, even our worth. But the fact that we noticed at all is sacred. It means we're awake. We're aware.

The Desert Fathers taught that awareness is the beginning of transformation. They didn't seek to eliminate fear; they sought to see it without flinching. And that's the key, observation without attachment. Seeing the fear, the doubt, the ego, noting it, and then letting it pass like crisp autumn light through the kitchen window.

This is how Musashi fought. Not with flourish, but with precision. He wrote, "Think lightly of yourself and deeply of the world." That's the posture of mastery.

Because clarity is our natural state. When we remove the fog of ego, fear, and attachment, what remains is presence. And presence moves. It doesn't hesitate. It doesn't cling. It doesn't perform. It simply responds. This is why Zen archers release their arrows without aiming.

Why do *aikido* masters blend with their adversary's attack without resistance? Why do great leaders speak truth without apology? They've trained the art of seeing clearly and moving cleanly. To observe without attachment and act without hesitation is not a technique. It's a way of being. It's how we train the invisible. How we move through life with clarity, courage, and grace.

So, whether you're in the boardroom, the *dojo*, the campsite, or the quiet of your own thoughts, remember this: See clearly. Move cleanly.

And let your life become the art.

Do Not Seek Comfort, Seek Clarity

> "If you look for truth, you may find comfort in the end. If you look for comfort, you will not get either comfort or truth, only soft soap and wishful thinking to begin, and in the end, despair."
>
> — C. S. Lewis

Do not seek comfort, seek clarity. It is a statement that is not a rejecting cause. It's a declaration of purpose. In a world that tempts us with distraction, softness, and sedation, this phrase is a compass. It points toward truth, even when truth is painful.

Many people find themselves drifting toward comfort. Not because they're weak, but because comfort is seductive. It whispers safety. It offers rest. It promises relief. But comfort, when sought as a goal, becomes a trap. It dulls the edge. It clouds the mirror. It replaces clarity with convenience.

In life, this shows up as avoiding the hard bumps, avoiding the hard conversations. We stay warm in our safe spaces, but we stop growing.

We're taught to chase comfort, better seats, faster service, smoother paths. Discomfort is framed as failure. Every advertisement, every commercial is about creating more comfort. Comfort you have a "right" to, and anything less is unacceptable. In the lower levels of behavior, discomfort is met with violence, riots, or mayhem.

Clarity often reveals what we'd rather not see, our limits, our contradictions, our unmet potential. Comfort hides it. Clarity exposes it. Lean into the sting, it makes you stronger.

When life feels heavy, comfort offers escape. It's easier to scroll than to reflect. Easier to repeat than to refine. But Musashi reminds us, "You must understand that there is more than one path to the top of the mountain." Clarity is not a single answer, rarely is there one. It's a merely a way of seeing. Without it we're lost.

When we realize we've been seeking comfort, it can feel disorienting. We might question our discipline, our direction, even our identity. But this moment, this noticing, is sacred. It means we're aware. Now we can do something about it.

The Desert Fathers taught that clarity begins with solitude. Not isolation, but intentional stillness. They didn't seek comfort. They sought communion with truth, with spirit, with self.

And that's the key: Clarity is not harsh. It's honest.

Because clarity is our natural state. When we remove the fog of distraction, fear, and sedation, what remains is presence. And presence is powerful. Presence doesn't need comfort. It doesn't fear discomfort. It simply sees. This is why Zen masters and Monks alike sit in silence. They're not seeking ease. They're seeking essence.

To seek clarity over comfort is not a rejection of rest. It's a commitment to truth. It's how we train the invisible. How we move through life with integrity, courage, and grace. So, whether you're at work or at home with your thoughts, remember this: Comfort may soothe, but clarity awakens.

And when you seek clarity, you don't just sharpen your practice. You illuminate your path.

Do not seek comfort. Seek clarity.

2. Master Your Voice and Shape the World

"The privilege of a lifetime is to become who you truly are."

— Carl Jung

Our second chapter emphasizes the power of intentional communication and the importance of using language to build clarity and authenticity rather than to mimic trends or sow confusion. You will learn to speak with precision, rhythm, and resonance, treating words as tools to shape reality and foster understanding. By aligning speech with values and purpose, you will elevate your communication, lead with integrity, and create a lasting impact through your words and deeds. Even the best ideas fall flat if you cannot adequately express them.

Speak as an Architect not an Echo

"The only person you are destined to become is the person you decide to be."

— Ralph Waldo Emerson

Speak as an architect, not echo. It's a call to build, not repeat. To shape thought, not mimic noise. To speak from the center of your experience, not the perimeter of someone else's.

In today's world, many voices sound alike, not necessarily because people lack insight, but because they've been trained to repeat. To echo trends, slogans, and borrowed ideas. It's how we're socialized, what we learn from our earliest days in school; critical thinking is rarely taught or appreciated. This shows up as parroting lineage without understanding. In leadership, it shows up as a quoting strategy without embodiment. In creative work, it shows up as mimicry disguised as homage.

The problem isn't a lack of intelligence. It's a surrender of authorship. We're surrounded by content, videos, posts, soundbites. It's easier to repeat than to reflect.

Speaking as an architect requires vulnerability. You might be misunderstood. You might stand alone. Don't fear originality. Most systems reward conformity. Echoes are safe. Architects are disruptive. But Lao Tzu reminds us: "Knowing others is intelligence; knowing yourself is true wisdom." To speak as an architect is to speak from wisdom.

When we realize we've been echoing, it can feel disorienting. We might question our voice, our value, even our identity. But this moment, this noticing, is sacred. In noticing we're far more aware than the masses who do not. The Desert Fathers taught that silence is the furnace of originality. They didn't speak often, but when they did, their words carried weight. Not because they echoed scripture, but because they embodied it.

And that's the key: speak from embodiment, not imitation. The solution is not to reject influence. It's to integrate it. Here are three ideas that, as an architect of your life, you may want to consider:

- Architects of life study. They learn from masters, but they don't mimic them.
- Architects of life speak slowly. They pause before responding. They ask themselves, "Is this mine?" before sharing.
- Architects of life shape space. Their words create room for others to think, feel, and grow.

This is how Musashi wrote. His *Dokkodo* wasn't a summary of others; it was a blueprint of his soul. As an example, he said, "Respect Buddha and the gods without counting on their help." Whether you agree with Musashi or not, that's the voice of an architect.

Your voice is already unique. It doesn't require permission. It wants presence. Your unique voice is waiting; you need to foster your voice. When you speak from clarity, not comfort, from experience, not echo, you become a builder of thought. And builders leave a legacy.

This is why Bruce Lee said, "Absorb what is useful, discard what is not, add what is uniquely your own." He didn't echo tradition. He reimagined it. He started with a strong foundation in classical *Wing Chun*, added boxing and fencing, and as his studies evolved through research, experimentation, and training with others, all focused on practical, efficient technique and application, he made *Jeet Kun Do* his own.

Develop a creed. Write your own guiding slogan. Something like, "I build my words from truth." "I shape my own thoughts with intention, not imitation." Or "I speak to create, not conform." This alone can evolve your mindset.

To speak as an architect is not to reject tradition. It's to honor it by building upon it. It's how we train the invisible. How we move through life with integrity, originality, and grace. So, whether you're in the *dojo* or the studio, sitting at your desk or the quiet of your own thoughts, remember this: Echoes fade. Architecture endures.

And when you speak as an architect, you don't just share your voice. You shape the world.

Use Language to Shape Reality not Decorate Confusion

"Make up your mind to leave the past and the old you behind. Focus on giving birth to a new you... the real you."

— Anonymous

Use language to shape reality, not to decorate confusion. It's a call to speak with precision. To teach with integrity. To lead with clarity. In a world that often rewards cleverness over coherence, this principle is a return to form.

People can fall into a trap: They use language to sound wise, rather than to be clear.

We hear it in overcomplicated instructions. We see it in vague mission statements. We feel it in conversations that leave us more confused than grounded. As Albert Einstein is often attributed as having said, "Any intelligent fool can make things more complicated, but it takes a touch of genius, and a lot of courage, to move in the opposite direction."

The problem isn't vocabulary. Its intention. Language becomes a veil instead of a window. A performance instead of a tool.

Sounding profound is rewarded more than being understood. This is a form of cultural performance. Complexity becomes a mask for authority. You need only look at a politician, any politician, to see how this format is used to appear as authority.

In *The Analects* Confucius wrote, "If language is not correct, then what is said is not what is meant. If what is said is not what is meant, then what ought to be done remains undone. If this remains undone, morals and art will deteriorate. If morals and art are corrupted, justice will go astray. If justice goes astray, the people will stand about in helpless confusion. Hence there must be no arbitrariness in what is said. This matters above everything."

This is not a metaphor. It is a warning. Have we not seen a decline into "helpless confusion" throughout many parts of society today? Simplicity requires commitment. It means choosing one idea and one truth. That's vulnerable because it can be understood.

When we realize we've been decorating confusion, using language to impress, distract, or avoid, it can feel disorienting. That is why using words to confuse is popular. George Orwell wrote of it in his classic book, *1984*, "War is peace." "Freedom is slavery." And "Ignorance is strength." These inverted phrases lead us to question our own voice.

But this moment, this realization, is sacred. It means when we see it, we're ready to speak from the center, not the surface.

The Desert Fathers believed that silence was the furnace of clarity. They didn't speak often, but when they did, their words cut through illusion. Not necessarily because they were eloquent, but because they were true.

This is how Musashi wrote. His *Dokkodo* wasn't poetic. It was precise. "Do not, under any circumstances, depend on a partial feeling." That's not decoration. That's the direction.

Because clarity is a practice.

When we align our language with our values, our experience, and our intention, we stop performing and start building. And when we build with words, we shape the world around us. This is why Zen koans are short. This is why military commands are crisp. And, it is why great leaders speak plainly.

They're not simplifying. They're sculpting.

Before teaching or responding, pause. Let the silence reveal what matters. This is the opposite of today's acts of talking over each other. As Stephen R. Covey sagely wrote, "Seek first to understand, then to be understood." Ask yourself at the end of your words, "Did this clarify or confuse?" This is a difficult but valuable act. Practice explaining a complex concept in one sentence. Your goal is not to reduce it, but rather to reveal its essence.

An example of this is from comedian Norm MacDonald. MacDonald believed the perfect joke would be where the setup and the punchline were identical. This wasn't about laziness; it was about purity. A kind of comedic minimalism, where the humor emerged from the truth of the statement itself.

To use language to shape reality is not a stylistic choice. It's a moral one. It's how we train the invisible. How we lead with integrity. So, whether you're in the classroom or the quiet of your own thoughts, remember this:

Speak to reveal. Speak to refine. Speak to awaken.

And when you do, your words won't decorate confusion. They'll carve clarity.

Speak Like You Move, Move Like You Speak

> "Your beliefs become your thoughts,
> your thoughts become your words,
> your words become your actions,
> your actions become your habits,
> your habits become your values,
> your values become your destiny."
>
> — Mahatma Gandhi

We learn to move in life with rhythm and significance. What if our words followed that same path? This is about elevating how we communicate, so our speech becomes as fluid as our walk.

Here's the challenge: Much of today's discourse is reactive, fragmented, and performative. We speak to win, not to understand. We interrupt rhythm with noise. We sacrifice clarity for cleverness. And in doing so, we lose the deeper connection that discourse can offer.

In life, poor movement leads to injury. In conversation, sloppy language leads to misunderstandings.

The problem isn't disagreement. The problem is dissonance. We're conditioned to respond quickly, not thoughtfully. Instant replies replace considered reflection. Blame the internet and the 24-hour news cycle for this need for instant response. Short bursts of opinion dominate. Rhythm is lost. Precision is optional.

We identify with our ideas, so critique feels personal. Listening becomes a threat. Marcus Aurelius wrote, "The impediment to action advances action. What stands in the way becomes the way." The same applies to speech. The obstacle, miscommunication, is the path to deeper clarity.

When we begin to elevate our discourse, however, something shifts. We slow down. We listen more. We speak less, but with greater impact. It can feel unfamiliar, even vulnerable. Precision requires presence. Rhythm requires patience. Resonance requires empathy.

It's hard. But this is where mastery begins.

Think of Musashi. His 60 duels weren't won by speed alone. They were won by timing, clarity, and presence. By strategy. His sword was an extension of his mind. Our words can be the same.

The solution is to treat speech like movement.

Say what you mean. No more, no less. Let your words breathe. Pause. Listen. Respond. Speak from depth, not volume. Let your words land. This isn't about being eloquent. It's about being intentional.

In *Art of War*, Sun Tzu wrote, "Words are easy, actions are hard." But when words become actions, when they carry weight, timing, and truth, they shape the battlefield of ideas.

When we elevate discourse, several things happen: We hear beyond the words. Precision removes ambiguity. Rhythm reduces tension. Resonance builds trust; as a result, people feel seen, not judged. Clear speech reflects clear thought.

This is how you should lead, not by force, but by presence, not by volume, but by vibration. Others follow clarity.

Here are a few ideas to begin:

- Choose an idea and explain it in three sentences to yourself. It is suggested you write these three sentences. Then refine it to one sentence. In conversation, let silence shape your rhythm. Don't rush the reply. Notice the rhythm in others' speech. Mirror it. Respect it.
- Choose a passage from Musashi, Aurelius, Lao Tzu, or The Bible. Read it slowly and aloud. Feel the weight of each word. Our words deserve discipline. Precision is clarity. Rhythm is presence. Resonance is impact.

So today, let's elevate our discourse. Let's speak deliberately, fluidly, and grounded. Because in the end, the way we speak is the way we lead. And the way we lead is the way we live.

Do Not Perform, Construct

"All colors will agree in the dark."

— Francis Bacon

Here is a meditation on a simple but powerful mind shift: move from performance to construction. In conversation and in life, we often find ourselves performing. Like actors, we mimic, we display, we react. But what happens when we stop performing and begin constructing?

This isn't about style. It's about substance. It's about building something real, something enduring, something that reflects who we are and what we stand for.

Here's the challenge: many people spend their energy performing rather than constructing. We perform for approval. We perform for tradition. We perform for the mirror, the audience, and the algorithm. But performance, by nature, is external. It's reactive. It's shaped by what others expect.

The word "perform" means to carry out an action or a task, such as dancing or playing an instrument, while "preform" means to shape or form something beforehand. That's construction. Construction is internal. It's deliberate. It's shaped by what we know to be true.

When we perform, we replicate. When we construct, we create.

From childhood, we're rewarded for appearances. Smiles, grades, trophies. The external becomes the measure. Visibility in social media becomes currency. We perform to be seen, not to be understood. Construction involves risk. Performance feels safer. It's rehearsed, predictable.

In *Meditations*, Marcus Aurelius reminds us, "Waste no more time arguing what a good man should be. Be one." That's construction. Not display. Not debate. But embodiment.

When we begin to shift from performance to construction, discomfort arises. We lose our applause. We lose the script. We lose the illusion of control. But we gain something deeper: authenticity. Integrity. Presence.

In the 20th century, Jigoro Kano transformed *jujutsu* into *judo*. Kano did this not to preserve tradition, but to construct a system of education, ethics, and evolution. He built something. And it lasted. Created in Japan in 1882, *judo* is a worldwide Olympic sport today.

When we construct rather than perform, several things happen. Growth becomes organic. We evolve from the inside out, not from external pressure. We're not dependent on applause, we're anchored in purpose. What we build endures. It teaches. It inspires.

William Shakespeare wrote in the play, *As You Like It*, "All the world's a stage, and all the men and women merely players." That is to be rejected out of hand; your life is not a play, it's architecture.

Every movement is a brick. Every breath is mortar. Every choice is a beam. So today, let's stop performing. Let's start constructing. Let's build something that lasts, within ourselves, within our communities.

Because in the end, what we build is who we become.

3. Build Your Life Brick by Brick

> "Creating a life that reflects your values and satisfies your soul is a rare achievement."
>
> — Bill Waterson

This third chapter focuses on building a life that reflects your personal values through deliberate systems and actions. Aligning daily practices, relationships, and working with core principles allows you to achieve authenticity and long-term growth. By promoting with boldness and serving with depth, you can live with precision and purpose, embodying your values, and focusing on meaningful causes rather than chasing fleeting outcomes. Here you will learn to become the architect of your life, constructing a legacy that will endure through intentionality, discipline, and alignment with your true self.

BUILDING WHAT REFLECTS YOUR VALUES

"THE WAY WE LIVE OUR DAYS IS
THE WAY WE LIVE OUR LIVES."

— ANNIE DILLARD

There comes a moment, often quiet and unannounced, when a person realizes they've been living in a structure not of their own making. It may be a career, a belief system, a social circle, or a daily rhythm. The walls feel familiar, but not true. You find yourself seeking something that reflects your values. This section is for those who have reached that moment and are ready to build something else, something more.

Marcus Aurelius reminds us that "The impediment to action advances action. What stands in the way becomes the way." The obstacle is not the enemy; it is the invitation. Building what reflects your values is not a retreat from the world. It is a deliberate engagement with the world. It is the act of shaping your life as a craftsman shapes wood, with clarity, force, and care, shaving away the unessential bits to reveal the beauty within.

The problem is not confusion. It is misalignment. Many live in tension between what they believe and what they build. Their work, relationships, and routines do not echo their convictions. Plato would call this a fracture between the soul and the *polis*. *Polis* is an ancient Greek word for "state," one which represents the philosophic ideal of political and social circumstances. Here we are using it in reference to the totality of you working in harmony with yourself.

Ayn Rand would call failure to live in internal and external harmony a failure to live as a "prime mover." Padre Pio might call it spiritual drift. This misalignment breeds fatigue, not the kind cured by a good night's sleep, but rather the kind that dulls the spirit. It shows up in quiet resignation, in the avoidance of mirrors, in the slow erosion of enthusiasm. The Desert Fathers saw this as *acedia,* a term which came from the Greek word for "lack of care," It manifests as a resistance to the demands of love and duty, leading to boredom, frustration, spiritual dissatisfaction, and despair. In other words, *acedia* is a spiritual weariness born of disconnection from your purpose.

Sound familiar?

The causes are many, but they share a common root, surrendering authorship. Descartes warned against accepting inherited truths without examination. Tony Robbins speaks of the "invisible scripts" that shape behavior. Musashi taught that the way is in training, intentional repetition, not passive absorption.

We inherit systems, expectations, and roles. We are taught to conform before we are taught to reflect. Baruch Spinoza would urge us to understand the causes of our emotions, not be ruled by them. Spinoza, in *Ethics,* laid out a view of human emotions, writing, "I have labored carefully, not to mock, lament, or execrate human actions, but to understand them."

The reaction to misalignment varies. Some retreat into silence, like St. Anthony. Others lash out, like Schopenhauer. Some build empires, some write, teach, mentor, or train. The reaction is not the solution, but it is the signal. It says, "Something is off." This is when we know that something must be built anew.

The reaction is the first draft. It is raw, but it is real. It must be shaped, not suppressed.

The problem is solved by reclaiming authorship. By building deliberately. By choosing materials that reflect your values, time, energy, relationships, work, and rituals. Marcus Aurelius wrote daily to remind himself of what mattered. Mike Mentzer trained with precision and intensity, rejecting excess. Ayn Rand built characters who lived by their own code.

You solve the problem by becoming the architect of your life. Not by tearing down what exists, but by constructing what must be.

The problem is solved because the builder has awakened. Because the values are no longer abstract, they are embodied. Because the structure begins to echo the soul. Spinoza would say that understanding leads to freedom. Plato would say that the form has been found. Robbins would say that identity has shifted.

To be clear, the solution is not external, it is internal expressed outward. Below are some action items to explore. As you review this action item list, keep in mind the words of British statistician George E. P. Box, "All models are wrong, but some are useful."

- Write your values in clear, active language. Review them regularly, at a cadence that suits your needs.
- Audit your calendar, relationships, and routines. Do they reflect your values?
- Choose one area, work, health, or creativity, and rebuild it from the ground up.
- Read daily from thinkers who challenge and clarify your convictions.
- Train your body and mind with discipline. Mentzer and Musashi agree: the way is physical.

- Speak your values aloud. Teach them. Live them.

Building what reflects your values is not a luxury. It is a necessity. It is the only way to live without fracture. The examined life must be expressed, not merely contemplated. This is a deeper invitation to build. Not with borrowed tools, but with your own. Not in reaction, but in creation.

The structure will be yours.

And it will stand.

Create Systems, Not Slogans

> "You do not rise to the level of your goals. You fall to the level of your systems."
>
> — James Clear

Create systems, not slogans. In a world flooded with catchphrases and motivational noise, we're going to dig deeper. We'll draw from a board of timeless minds, Marcus Aurelius, Miyamoto Musashi, Baruch Spinoza, Ayn Rand, Padre Pio, and others. Our goal is to build a framework that actually works.

This isn't about rejecting inspiration. It's about replacing abstraction with architecture. Let's begin…

We live in an age of slogans. "Unlock your true potential." "Think positive." "Hustle harder." These phrases are everywhere, on mugs, shirts, and social feeds. They sound good. They feel good. But they don't actually build anything.

Marcus Aurelius warned against being, "A man of many words and few deeds." Musashi said, "Do nothing which is of no use." Slogans are often of no use. They're noise without structure. They do not train the mind, they do not shape behavior, and by their very shallowness they do not endure.

In a culture of immediacy, slogans offer fast relief. Schopenhauer called this, "The illusion of understanding."

Bishop Barron reminds us that spiritual maturity requires wrestling with complexity. Do not bypass complexity with platitudes.

Don Draper, portrayed by actor Jon Hamm, is the protagonist of the show *Mad Men*. He understood branding. Slogans sell. But selling isn't solving. Ayn Rand saw slogans as tools of collectivism, ways to obscure individual accountability, writing, "The uncontested absurdities of today are the accepted slogans of tomorrow."

Slogans are easy to repeat. Systems require effort, reflection, and design. A system is what you are building now.

The reaction to this realization can be sobering. You might feel exposed. You might recognize how many slogans you've internalized. That's okay.

St. Anthony retreated to the desert not to escape, but to confront. Padre Pio endured suffering not to be pitied, but to be purified. Systems begin with silence, with solitude, with the willingness to see clearly.

Chris Langan would say, "The system is the story." If your life is a story, what's the structure? What's the rhythm? What's the repeatable process?

The solution is to build systems, repeatable, resilient, reality-based frameworks. Here are a few examples:

- Mike Mentzer built his training philosophy on intensity, recovery, and logic, not hype. Mentzer was the first bodybuilder to receive a perfect score. And he did it way back in 1978, in the IFBB Mr. Universe competition.

- Spinoza taught that freedom comes from understanding causes, not reacting to symptoms. Spinoza's framework offers a bridge between Stoic discipline and mystical insight. In Spinoza's world, emotions are signals to be understood and integrated.

- Plato designed the republic as a system of justice, not a slogan of fairness.
- Tony Robbins teaches rituals, not rah-rah. Morning routines, priming, journaling, these are systems foundational to personal and professional growth.

Systems solve problems because they endure. They adapt. They scale. They succeed because systems engage the whole person, mind, body, and spirit. Systems create feedback loops. They expose weaknesses, and they evolve with you.

Musashi's *Go Rin No Sho* (*Book of Five Rings*) is a system of combat and consciousness. Descartes' method of doubt is a system of inquiry. The Desert Fathers lived systems of prayer, fasting, and reflection. These weren't slogans. They were scaffolding for transformation.

Let's make this real. Here's how:

- Write down the phrases you repeat and then ask yourself, "Do these guide my behavior"?
- Design a morning system: Include movement, reflection, and intention. Keep it consistent. A constituency has its own volume. Embrace the long haul.
- Use principles, not moods. Define your filters, then review your week. What worked? What didn't? Adjust.
- Systems thrive in aligned spaces. Declutter. Simplify. Optimize.

Marcus Aurelius didn't write slogans. He wrote meditations. Musashi didn't preach. He practiced.

Spinoza didn't moralize. He modeled. Your life deserves more than a catchphrase. It deserves a system.

So today, begin. Build something that lasts. Not for applause. Not for branding. But for mastery.

Promote with Boldness, Serve with Depth

> "Those who are happiest are those who do the most for others."
>
> — Booker T. Washington

We live in a time where visibility is currency. But visibility without substance is erosion. The people mentioned in this book or quoted herein offer a unified message: Boldness must be rooted in service. Promotion must be anchored in depth.

The problem is not ambition. The problem is hollow ambition.

We see it everywhere: loud voices, big claims, shallow follow-through. The world rewards noise, but noise doesn't nourish. Bishop Barron warns of the, "Culture of self-display," where the soul is traded for attention. Ayn Rand saw this as the triumph of second-handers. Second-handers are those who seek approval without achievement.

Why does this happen? The ego fears obscurity, but visibility without value becomes spectacle.

Fedor Vladimirovich Emelianenko once said, "Many confuse silence with weakness," An MMA fighter who amassed an impressive record of 40 wins, 7 losses, and 1 no contest, Fedor's appeal wasn't just his accomplishments in the ring, it was his presence. He rarely showed emotion and never taunted his opponents.

Tony Robbins teaches that people are conditioned to seek certainty and significance. Promotion offers both certainty and significance, temporarily. The reaction to this realization can be sobering. You may feel exposed. You may see your own patterns, moments of self-promotion without substance.

Padre Pio said, "Pray, hope, and don't worry." That's not a slogan. It's a system of surrender and action. Spinoza taught that freedom comes from understanding causes. This moment is a cause. Your reaction is the beginning of clarity.

Speak clearly. Share your work. Stand in your truth. Plato taught that the soul thrives in the light. Build systems. Offer value. Mentor. Schopenhauer said, "Talent hits a target no one else can hit. Genius hits a target no one else can see." To serve with depth is to aim for the unseen.

Depth creates durability. And boldness creates reach.

Descartes taught us to doubt, then to build. The Desert Fathers taught us to retreat, and then to return. Promotion without depth fades. Depth without promotion hides. Integration solves the problem because it reflects reality: we are meant to be seen and to serve.

Promote with boldness. Serve with depth. After all, as Tony Robbins wrote, "People who fail focus on what they have to go through; people who succeed focus on what it will feel like at the end."

Speak boldly. Serve deeply. Build systems.

Live visibly. Act meaningfully.

Live with Precision and Purpose

> "He who has a 'why' to live for
> can bear almost any how."
>
> — Friedrich Nietzsche

The problem is hesitation. Not silence, but the kind of hesitation that comes from second-guessing your value. Many creators, leaders, and mentors hold back not because they lack skill, but because they fear being misunderstood, rejected, or perceived as self-serving.

Marcus Aurelius warned, "You could leave life right now. Let that determine what you do and say and think." Boldness is not vanity. It's an urgency.

Why do we hesitate?

Bishop Barron speaks of a culture that rewards spectacle but punishes sincerity. Know this, you will suffer the punishment for your sincerity, and more often than not it will come as cruelty wrapped in the vilest hatred. But that doesn't mean you should put on a false front, hold yourself back. Living with precision and purpose means leaning in to your value, your truth.

When you realize you've been holding back, the reaction can be sharp. You may feel regret. You may feel exposed. That's good. That's the beginning of motion.

Seneca spoke about the value of a purpose driven life thousands of years ago, writing, "Let all your efforts be directed to something, let it keep that end in view. It is not activity that disturbs people, but false conceptions of things that drive them mad."

Hesitation is of no use. Ayn Rand would call it a betrayal of self. Tony Robbins would call it a failure of state. Elon Musk would call it a design flaw. Now that you see it, you need to fix it.

The solution is to promote with boldness, not as a performance, but as a principle. Plato taught that the soul thrives in truth. Speak clearly. Mike Mentzer built his training system on logic and intensity. Promote your work with the same precision.

Spinoza reminds us, "The more you struggle to live, the more you realize that life is joy." Boldness is a form of joy.

Boldness aligns with reality. It reflects your actual contribution, and it invites others into your system. It creates momentum.

Boldness becomes easier when it's built on truth, system, and service. To promote with boldness is to live with alignment. Musashi would nod in silence. Spinoza would smile in clarity. Tony Robbins would shout in energy. Padre Pio would pray in gratitude.

You are here to build, to serve, to speak. Promote with boldness. Not for applause. Not for branding. But for mastery.

Embody the Cause, Do Not Chase the Effects

"Be the ball, Danny."

— Ty Webb (played by Chevy Chase in *CADDYSHACK*)

Embody the cause, do not chase the effects. We will move through a simple map: Identify the problem, examine root causes, and choose a disciplined reaction.

People pursue outcomes as if outcomes were lodestars, the courses. In life, attention fixes on recognition, profit, praise, or avoiding discomfort. This trajectory fragments attention. It produces performance that is brittle under pressure and ethics that bend toward expedience. The result? A life that looks active but is truly hollow, a path that lacks sustained direction.

Several dynamics create the pursuit of effects.

Goals that are defined by external validation become fragile. The target shifts as public attention moves. Your goals are determined by the mob. The mob, whether physical or cyber, is no more intelligent than the base needs the mob wants to satisfy. Instant gratification, often fomented by chatbots and artificial intelligence, it's never real.

Shortcut culture. Systems reward rapid signals, likes quick wins, and viral moments. Behavior adapts to rewards. We are predators by nature. We desire quick fixes with low energy expenditure. It's in our genes.

Identity fragmentation. Without a grounded sense of purpose, people adopt whichever identity earns them immediate benefits. This can be seen in professional sports; everybody loves a winner yet walks away from the loser even when it's "their" team. Fairweather fans. Fairweather friends. These shifts of support, or fandom, are seasonal and mercurial.

History shows similar patterns. Consider the Roman legions that prized spoils over discipline. A single victory driven by plunder undermined long-term cohesion. In contrast, leaders who emphasized discipline produced institutions that lasted centuries. In an extreme example, General Crassus, renown for defeating Spartacus's slave army, used decimation (executing one of every ten men) to punish legions accused of cowardice, demonstrating that a focus on self-preservation and plunder over duty required brutal measures to correct.

Across time, philosophers and warriors alike proclaim the virtue of embodying a cause. Musashi taught an orientation of preparedness. Marcus Aurelius wrote about duty as a form of presence. Spinoza appealed to the power of understanding to align action with flourishment. These teachings point toward a deeper axis. Inhabit the cause, allow effects to flow from fidelity.

Adopt a practice-centered life. Make technique and character the objective. Train according to this principle. Choose methods that build durability and integrity. The corrective posture includes these commitments:

- Small practices, done daily, are necessary to reinforce identity.
- Use rituals. Rituals can reconnect action to purpose, an essential reinforcement loop.
- Understand that slow cycles of refinement are sustainable and aid in long-term growth.

This reaction resembles a fighter returning to fundamental drills after suffering a loss in the ring. The aim is steady recalibration, not dramatic overhaul. Schopenhauer's clarity about the seriousness of life supports disciplined focus. The Desert Fathers' rhythms of solitude and communal practice shape a consistent interior. Mike Mentzer's insistence on precise, intense work guides how to allocate effort.

Commitment to practice removes the hectic pace of chasing outcomes. You become available to the present task. You are neither living in the past nor drifting into the future, but focusing on the present. As a result, effects become byproducts of sustained discipline.

Build practices that embody the values you aim to express. Train habits that encode intention into "muscle memory," your brain's ability to perform activities automatically without conscious thought. This converts aspiration into reliable action.

Practice shapes capacity. Repetition of principled actions rewires both neural pathways and social expectations. Muscular memory and cultural habits operate on similar logic. As the body learns what the mind rehearses, communities learn what their rituals repeat. The essence of culture, after all, is shared story.

Daily practice directs attention into stable patterns. Attention is the currency of change. Habits focused on cause redirect attention away from transient rewards. Small, reliable wins strengthen commitment and scale slowly into systems.

Historical precedents are abundant. Plato's Academy designed space and ritual to create lifelong learners, a practice continued to this very day. Roman engineers reshaped habits through roads and baths. Modern entrepreneurs shape behavior by designing products with clear affordances. Each case shows how cause-driven design channels energy into durable results.

A few actions to speed your journey:

- Treat embodying the cause not chasing the effects like a training regimen. Work this theme into a 90-day cycle and record the changes as you make them.

- Inventory your habits. Keep a daily log for seven days. Note activities that support the sentence and those that drift away from it. This is reconnaissance.

- Create three micro-rituals. This is an enjoyable act as the rituals are your choice and are small, so small that others will probably not perceive them.

In this fashion, practice becomes destiny. When identity centers on principle, the body, the environment, and the circle around you adapt. Effects appear as reliable outcomes of disciplined living.

Musashi said, "You must understand that there is more than one path to the top of the mountain." Choose a path forged by faithful practice. Let obstacles you face along the way refine your method, but never stray from the goal.

Embody the cause.

4. Step Back to Level Up

> "Nowhere can man find a quieter
> or more untroubled retreat
> than in his own soul."
>
> – Marcus Aurelius

Our fourth chapter explores the transformative power of intentional retreat as a tool for refinement and growth. Retreat is not avoidance, but rather a disciplined practice to cultivate clarity, refine skills, and align oneself with purpose. By withdrawing from the noise of constant activity, you can nourish your inner life, confront challenges, and recalibrate your focus. Structured retreats paired with deliberate reentry to allow for deeper self-awareness, resilience, and mastery. The chapter highlights the importance of balancing solitude with service, using withdrawal to sharpen your capacities so that you can return to the world with renewed purpose and vigor.

Retreat to Refine, Return with Resolve

> "Truth, like gold, is to be obtained not by its growth, but by washing away from it all that is not gold."
>
> — Leo Tolstoy

Retreat to refine, return with resolve. This section treats withdrawal as an active, disciplined phase of training and of life. You are going to look at a purposeful retreat that polishes skill, attention, and character so that you are able to return to the world with clear intent and calibrated force. We'll move through an identification of what's broken, why it happens, a disciplined reaction, a central takeaway, and why that approach works.

People often pursue constant motion that looks like progress yet fails to deepen their capacity. Schedules fill with tasks, notifications multiply, and public performance crowds out private honing of one's craft. In life, the crowding out shows as an activity that amplifies noise while the internal stagnates.

Outcomes arrive sporadically and feel unstable. Presence fragments. Decisions become reactive. The result is a surface-level competence that falters under pressure paired with a spirit that grows thin from continual exposure.

Several forces conspire to hollow practice. The first of these is rewarding immediate demonstration over slow cultivation. We, by nature, steer our energy toward what is novel rather than what is necessary. Think of it as a, "What was that?" response to an unexpected noise. Fear of loss or delay pushes people away from solitude and rigorous rehearsal. As humans we are genetically built on a fear-of-loss platform.

These dynamics produce a chaotic world. Historical patterns repeat. Armies that prioritize parade over drill lose cohesion in the field. Spiritual traditions that neglect contemplative withdrawal lose clarity of purpose.

To alter this dynamic, retreat must become intentional practice. Retreating is not avoidance; it is methodical cultivation. To successfully retreat, you need to set the table correctly. First, set a timeframe and treat it as a committed training block. Establish a routine that includes solitude, study, and high-quality repetition. This one more, vital part of this process, which is to create accountability through an elder, peer, or recording system.

The problem resolves through cyclical attention. It doesn't matter what skill you're honing, be it application of a martial art or a TEDx talk, this two-fold action is comprised of withdrawal to cultivate depth followed by return to apply refined capacities. Structure your life in repeating seasons that alternate concentrated inward work with outward application. Each retreat deepens the foundation, each return tests adjustments in real-world conditions. Over time, this cycle yields resilience, precision, and a stable center.

Historically, effective leaders and practitioners follow this rhythm. Musashi's year-long retreats to isolate technique; Marcus Aurelius's morning solitude for daily resolve; Plato's academy creating time and space for thinking that reshaped public life. Each of these examples shows retreat as a productive phase that seeds stronger action.

Focused practice in low-noise environments allows neural circuits to form with higher fidelity. Solitude creates space to test assumptions and refine aims. When motives and values are clearer, choices in action become simpler and more aligned. A refined aim concentrates effort; energy no longer leaks into contradictory pursuits.

This cycle of refinement and application compounds. Skill deepens, judgment sharpens, courage stabilizes.

Musashi said, "From one thing, know ten thousand things." A retreat that focuses on fundamentals multiplies applicability.

Marcus Aurelius began each day with a practice of interior preparation and closed every day in examination. His routine demonstrates retreat's power to shape conduct, even when each period of retreat lasts for a short time. Similarly, St. Benedict set rhythms of work and silence that allowed monastic communities to hold discipline over the centuries. A modern example: A coach who withdraws his team to a mountain camp for focused practice and subsequently returns with players who hold their composure under pressure.

Mike Mentzer's philosophy of intensity and economy appears here as a call for concentrated, high-quality training blocks. Spinoza's emphasis on understanding as the source of joy shows how clarity produced in retreat becomes the fuel for sustained resolve and performance.

Retreat to refine, return with resolve is a discipline that marries solitude and service. Withdrawal is an instrument for sharpening capacity; return is the environment where the sharpened instrument proves its worth. Train this cycle into your routine. Keep your objectives clear, your rituals precise, and your feedback honest.

Three practical reminders to carry into your next cycle.

- Name your refinement objective in a single, clear sentence and repeat it daily.
- Test it in the world.
- Find a time and a place for a small, micro test of your daily reminder.

Close your eyes, take a breath, and sharpen one skill. Do it today. Prepare to return with a resolve that speaks in deeds. Rinse and repeat.

Retreat for Many Reasons

"I am not a product of my circumstances.
I am a product of my decisions."

— Stephen R. Covey

People retreat for many reasons. Sometimes it is fatigue, embarrassment, or fear. When retreat becomes avoidance, training stalls, relationships fray, and insight dims. The problem is a habitual retreat that blurs into silence without purpose. It's withdrawal that conceals the issue rather than illuminating it, situational, cognitive, or emotional avoidance that can manifest as dysfunctions such as procrastination, perfectionism, or anxiety disorders.

In life after a loss, we naturally want to avoid others who expose our weakness. We shrink from honest feedback. Another marker of retreat is pausing conversations that need resolution. The phrase, "I don't want to talk about it," is an indicator of retreating. Retreat means postponing hard decisions, isolating ourselves with a vain hope that problems will evaporate on their own.

Several forces conspire to turn healthy withdrawal into evasion. And there is a profound difference between healthy withdrawal and detrimental avoidance.

When skill is tied to self-worth, failure feels like an existential threat. Failure is you, and you are the failure. Stepping back becomes a shelter from perceived judgment whether it truly exists or not. Your identity, your pride, it is all wrapped up in your performance. Fail a test, lose a competition, miss a goal, squander a promotion, and rather than learning a way to improve and prevail your sense of self diminishes.

Without conscious practice on how to withdraw, people slip into patterns. These patterns are shaped by emotion instead of purpose. Emotions are an outside force to be understood, not hidden from. Facing the gap between how we appear and what we can do requires courage. Avoidance is emotionally safer in the short term, but dysfunctional over the long run.

Avoidance only forestalls the inevitable arrival of the problem. And when the inevitable appears, it shows up in full force.

After the Battle of Hastings, in which King Harold II of England was killed, Edgar Ætheling, the last surviving male member of the royal house of Cerdic of Wessex, was elected King by the Witan (council of elders) but never crowned. Edgar and other English lords and bishops withdrew to London to consider their next move but their deliberation ultimately ended with surrender to William the Conqueror as they believed they could not defeat him in battle. William then marched on London, was crowned king on Christmas Day in 1066, and ruled until his death in 1087.

Edgar and his cohorts retreated and reviewed their situation. They chose to ponder their options in the calm of London. Ultimately, they chose no more war. When faced with unclear withdrawal, they responded with curiosity and contemplation rather than judgment, knowing that the immediate emotional reactions of shame, relief, anger, or the desire for protracted battle deserved recognition and a clear decision.

Emotional reactions are data. They indicate what values, expectations, or fears were triggered. Observe them. Note the story your mind tells you about the event. Ask yourself, "Am I stepping back to solve or to disappear"?

As you can see, a quiet, disciplined reaction transforms a reflex into a tool.

The problem is resolved when withdrawal is made deliberately and in a structured way. Withdrawal becomes clarifying when it follows a clear protocol: (1) Pause, (2) Diagnose, (3) Refine, and (4) Return. This is a loop, an intentional micro-cycle that any practitioner can run after a setback or overload.

Here's how it works:

- Pause with full attention.
- Name the reason for withdrawal in specific terms.
- Decide on a short, measurable objective for the pause.
- Use the pause to gather one corrective insight.
- Re-enter with a concrete, limited action.

Applying this protocol to Edgar Ætheling and the English lord's challenges in 1066, we find the following:

- We lost the battle and our king is dead.
- William is on his way to London; we need to fight or flee.
- Can we defeat William?
- No, we don't have enough might to win a battle against William.
- Our best course is to appear before William and offer surrender to his conditions.

This protocol transforms retreat from omission into an essential part of mastery. Making withdrawal procedural converts a chaotic habit into a deliberate strategy. Structure brings clarity because it replaces fleeing with mapping. Mapping reduces cognitive load and restores personal agency. When you can name the reason for stepping back, interrupt the emotional spiral, and return with one focused adjustment, the reasoning tightens.

Philosophically, withdrawal aligned with purpose echoes Sun Tzu's admonition, "The supreme art of war is to subdue the enemy without fighting." Withdrawal here is a strategic repositioning to gain information, conserve resources, and exploit a larger advantage. In practice, it cultivates humility and curiosity, qualities necessary for sustained progress.

Musashi wrote of disciplined solitude, withdrawing into practice without distraction in order to form judgment and technique. Solitude, used well, reveals what the body knows yet the mind denies. Marcus Aurelius counseled returning to first principles when overwhelmed, tightening attention on what is within your control.

Miyamoto Musashi's later years were marked by intentional withdrawal into study and practice that clarified a lifetime of combat into crisp technique and formidable philosophy. That's how he was able to codify his winning strategies in *Go Rin No Sho*, and a large part of the reason why we know his name today. After all, while his duel with Saski Kojiro on Ganryu Island was one of the most famous events in Japanese history, few remember the name of the guy he killed there.

These examples show withdrawal functioning as refinement. The purpose is clarity, an engineered reentry that leaves confusion behind.

Withdrawal becomes a refining tool when it is practiced with intention, limited scope, and clear measures. Make pauses into experiments: Test one variable, gather the result, and return to practice. The work of mastery requires the courage to face what we lack and the discipline to turn retreat into insight.

The adage, "When stepping back, I will step back to see," resonates. You may retreat for many reasons. Make sure they're intentioned and intentional ones.

Nourish the Soul Before Raising the Voice

> "Take calculated risks. That is quite different from being rash."
>
> — George S. Patton

Nourish the soul before raising the voice. Marcus Aurelius wrote, "You have power over your mind, not outside events. Realize this, and you will find strength." Use that line as a promise: Tending the inner life changes everything that follows.

Often, people perform, speak, and push from a place of depletion. Anger becomes authority. Quick reactions replace considered counsel. Training, work, social media, and perceived urgency come together to erode tenderness and clarity. Resulting decisions feel loud and brittle. The problem shows up in classrooms, boardrooms, and kitchen tables alike.

The rhythm of modern life, with constant activity, fragments a person's attention. This incessant activity also starves us of reflection. The direct result of fragmentation and starvation is an over-reliance on external validation. Applause and metrics substitute for inner measure. This is not new. The classic film-noir, *Sunset Boulevard*, was made in 1950, three-quarters of a century ago as of this writing. That movie addressed the limits a person might go to in order to reclaim their fame, even murdering another human being.

Breathe. Refuse escalation. Replace immediate rebuttal with a two-step ritual: A one-minute inward check and a single clarifying question. Model this behavior aloud. For example, as a businessperson you might receive a rude email from an aggrieved customer. Rather than replying at high volume, flaming them back, it is far better to wait, breathe, review the facts, and respond with a calm correction that simultaneously educates and restores dignity.

This represents your company in a professional manner that can stand the light of day and may even change the angry person's mind. After all, the way we respond to complaints can solidify relationships or alienate customers for life, so make a conscious choice.

Tony Robbins wrote, "It is in your moments of decision that your destiny is shaped." Frame the pause as a decision that cultivates destiny. A personal, instrumental intention.

Consider the pause protocol by asking yourself, "Does this need to be reacted to right now?" If not, let it cool down, give the moment time to breathe, and then cast reaction to the side and respond. Never react with anger. Choose when and how to respond instead. Responding means taking control of a situation, whereas reacting cedes control to others.

Nourish the soul through practices that build steadiness, empathy, and clarity. When the inner life is tended, the voice that emerges has authority, warmth, and precision. The solution is a practical, repeatable regimen that transforms instinctive reaction into intentional response.

The soul responds to regular discipline. Marcus Aurelius taught that inner governance reshapes responses to external events. Spinoza's ethic locates freedom in understanding causes and aligning action with reason.

Practical training leads to habitual calm. Try the pause protocol for a week and watch your decision-making process change.

Habituating the pause protocol asserts control over yourself and ultimately, to the extent feasible, over the world. Never react, always respond. Nourish the soul before raising the voice.

5. Own Your Truth, Leave Your Mark

> "THE GREAT USE OF LIFE IS TO SPEND IT FOR SOMETHING THAT WILL OUTLAST IT."
>
> — WILLIAM JAMES

Our final chapter focuses on accepting reality and shaping a meaningful legacy through intentional action and alignment with your principles. You will learn that it is vital to lean into challenges rather than avoiding or denying them, using conflict as a tool for growth and understanding. Slow down and analyze systems before critiquing them, moving toward virtue and truth rather than following the irrationality of the crowd. By embracing reality, addressing obstacles with clarity, and prioritizing meaningful contributions over external validation, you can create a lasting impact that transcends fleeting recognition.

Accept Reality, Shape Legacy

> "Humility means accepting reality
> with no attempt to outsmart it."
>
> — David Richo

Accept reality, shape legacy. Those four words are the compass and a charge. Too many of us live in versions of life that are softened or distorted. We avoid hard facts, postpone decisions, and shape our days around distractions that feel comfortable.

Over time, small evasions accumulate into careers stalled, relationships frayed, and influence that evaporates. The problem is not failure; the problem is steady misalignment between what is true and what we act upon. We are subject to the fear of discomfort, loss, or pain. Our values are borrowed from popular culture. They are convenient and unprincipled. We tend to see setbacks as proof of our limits instead of necessary data for recalibration and growth.

When reality slaps you awake, three reactions commonly appear, (1) denial, (2) resignation, or (3) engagement:

- Denial rewrites facts into softer stories. Often this narrative carries an element of external blame, "I could of [xxxx], if only that manager hadn't blocked my promotion."

- Resignation collapses the purpose to a comfortable, warm robe of premature acceptance. There is a

Japanese saying, "*Shoganai,*" which means, "It cannot be helped." In English, we would say, with a shrug, "Wadda ya gunna do?"

- Engagement is the higher-level thinking. Engagement studies the facts, honestly names the obstacles, and activates action. It forms the basis for continuous improvement.

Clearly, enlightened folks choose engagement. But it's hard.

Think of leaders who faced constraints but used them for creative problem solving. For example, in 1315 Duke Leopold I of Austria sought to enforce the will of the Habsburg dynasty of the Swiss. He arrived with several thousand soldiers, including mounted knights and infantry. The Swiss, numbering about one thousand men and with no real hope of winning on paper, used creative maneuvers and terrain to defeat the Habsburgs. This secured the beginning of Swiss independence. Simply put, constraints of numbers were overcome.

Julian of Norwich was an anchoress in England during the 14th century. An anchoress was someone who lived in a cell attached to a church, a woman who chose a solitary, enclosed life of prayer and religious devotion. Nevertheless, Julian wrote *Revelations of Divine Love*, the earliest surviving book in English by a woman and a cornerstone of Christian mysticism. She turned constraints of gender, mobility, and conversation inward, leaving a legacy that survives to this day.

Here is a suggestion to assist you in accepting reality and shaping your future. Write three facts about a situation that you cannot change this week. Write three variables you can influence. This makes the landscape explicit. With an explicit landscape, you can take action. This is creative problem-solving.

Accept reality, shape legacy is not a slogan. It's a technique for life that refuses to drift. See the truth of your circumstances. Choose boldly, train patiently, live with clarity, act with integrity and you can leave something behind that outlasts your comforts.

The present is a narrow gate that opens to a wide field. By accepting reality, you can create legacy.

Turn Conflict into Opportunity

> "The quality of our lives depends not on whether or not we have conflicts, but on how we respond to them."
>
> — Thomas Crum

Conflict, how to prepare for it, respond when it arrives, and turn friction into forward motion. Conflict is not a failure of design; it is another form of signal. Read it, shape it, and harness it. Conflict then becomes one of your more reliable instructors.

Conflicts arise from relationships, are found all throughout organizations, and are endemic to creative work. The most insidious type of conflict, however, is inside your head. Conflict shows up as stalled projects, heated meetings, or silent resentments.

The problem is not the presence of disagreement. The problem is unpreparedness. Followed by uncertainty about principles. Emotional reactivity makes the situation worse.

Here is a quick list of potential issues that can lead to conflict: When values and objectives are vague, disputes become fights. Conflicts arise when two coherent wills meet without a common method for resolution. Suffering and unmet need are part of pain, fear, and longing. Suffering distorts judgment and inflates small slights into moral crises.

Most conflicts, even physical ones before they're fully engaged, can be resolved by using the threefold pause protocol: Pause, cool down, respond. Don't react. It is possible to talk your way out the vast majority of situations you can expect to face in life. According to the Bureau of Justice Statistics, the average U.S. citizen has about a 1.08% chance of facing violence perpetrated by a stranger and such incidents usually start with a verbal altercation. Deescalation stems from response, escalation from reaction.

Ask yourself, "Does this need to be reacted to right now?" If not, let it cool down, give the moment time to breathe, and then cast reaction to the side and respond. Assess, slow down cognitive and emotional escalation so that you don't exacerbate the problem. Marcus Aurelius recommends observing facts without immediate judgment. Ask yourself what is true, what is imagined, who benefits from escalation.

When institutions or people lack agreed principles for resolving their differences, reactions fragment into cycles of violence and revenge. This is nothing new. The dynamic is as old as history.

For example, after Caesar's assassination, Rome fractured. There was no clear, legitimate path for succession. Mark Antony used his position to rally forces in Rome. Octavian (Caesar's heir) entered the contest. Brutus and Cassius withdrew to the East and prepared for war. The result was open military confrontation at Philippi in 42 BC. A breakdown of Senatorial authority into military command and personal patronage also took place, compounding the challenges.

Contrast this dynamic with the centralized rule and practice of the Benedictine monks. The Rule of St. Benedict addresses petty conflicts with clear structure. How small can the rule go? The Rule of St. Benedict expressly forbids any monk from striking another brother. Chapter 70 of the Rule of St. Benedict states that striking another monk is strictly forbidden unless the abbot gives express permission.

A quote attributed to Confucius states, "What you do not want done to yourself, do not do to another." Adhering to this Golden Rule, conflict can be beneficial when it is harnessed to foster personal growth, stimulate creativity, or drive innovation. It avoids groupthink when problem-solving by leveraging diverse perspectives to achieve the best outcome from any given problem.

Conflict is solved by building a framework that converts friction into information and ultimately into forward momentum. When you remove noise, reactivity, and unclear aims, you reveal the heart of the problem that needs solving.

Marcus Aurelius teaches that obstacles become the path. Schopenhauer and Dostoevsky insist on attending to the interior causes of action.

History proves it. The Desert Fathers contained tensions by setting clear rules and a rhythm of obedience. Even today, business leaders who establish Responsibility, Authority, and Accountability (RAA) rules and set clear Key Performance Indicators (KPIs) often kill disputes before they even start. The most common causes of conflict in the workplace stem from ambiguous policies, unclear or incompatible goals, competition for resources, poor communication, and dysfunctional metrics rather than from leadership style or personality differences.

Expect conflict and prepare for it. By aligning principles, clarifying roles, training your inner life, and scripting responses, you transform friction into a reliable mechanism for discerning truth and driving personal growth.

Blunt tactical clarity of bold leaders informs you how you meet disagreement. Abraham Lincoln used plain language during the American Civil War. Before appointing Ulysses S. Grant, Lincoln said he wanted "A general who will fight." Grant gave Lincoln what he wanted by using unrelenting offense to win his battles.

Conflict will come. When it does, meet it with purpose, steadiness, and a plan.

Understand Systems before Critiquing Them

"If one does not understand a person, one tends to regard him as a fool."

— Carl Jung

The problem is fast critique without sufficient understanding. Surface impressions dominate the evaluation of organizations, policies, movements, and technologies. This critique of surface can result in misdiagnosis, bad solutions, and wasted effort. The pattern of surface critique appears in politics, business, media, sports, and personal relationships.

Marcus Aurelius taught that obstacles reveal the structure beneath them. When we rush to judgment, we miss that revelation. We fail to look under the boulder we find in our way.

Today's attention economy demands that we make instant decisions. These snap judgements can be seen as adroit, smart, or insightful when oftentimes they are not. Speed is valued over depth, even if it is a poor choice. Fairness is a child's idea. Yet we often use the passion of fairness as a tool to force a quick decision using moral urgency. Faux moral urgency married with a juvenile's emotion. This is what politicians use to get what they want. And we fall for it time and time again.

This challenge is exacerbated by specialization. If you show a rash to your doctor, a general practitioner, they will suggest you see a dermatologist. The modern world breaks life into specialties that don't generally communicate well, so we focus on symptoms without resolving the underlying problem.

Continuing along the lines of communication, the louder the voice, the better. More will listen. Add to that loudness a certainty of speech, a popular or pedigreed speaker, and we have a recipe for pure ego feed. It feels good, but accomplishes little.

Here are some powerful thoughts on the topic of understanding systems before critiquing them:

- Set aside emotions. Schopenhauer warns about will overpowering reason. He believed that when the desire to condemn dominates thought, reasoning collapses.

- Challenge assumptions. Descartes insists on methodical doubt: clear premises yielding robust conclusions.

- Lead with strategy. Musashi teaches the strategy of knowing the rhythm and timing of a system before striking.

- Look for the root cause. Spinoza models reasoned understanding of causes. A person should have clarity about how things follow from necessity prevents error.

- Slow down and center. Marcus Aurelius prescribes inner mastery. Before speaking, align judgment with principle.

- Practice listening to the people inside the system. The Desert Fathers showed a practice of humility and contemplative attention.

- Ask structural questions rather than moral headlines. Tony Robbins suggests shifting from problem statements to possibility-focused inquiries. These possibility-focused questions reveal control points.

- Avoid the trap of moral superiority. Dostoevsky's novels show that moral certainty without empathy makes one blind to complexity.
- Seek competence and evidence. Ayn Rand valued knowledge of facts and causal chains. Correct critique requires expertise and clarity.

Systems literacy works because systems are structured, not random. If you learn the architecture, the actors, incentives, constraints, feedback loops, and timing, your critique becomes diagnostic instead of performative.

Understanding systems before critiquing them is both an ethic and a craft. It asks us to slow down without losing urgency, to combine moral imagination with discipline. This discipline synthesizes ancient wisdom and modern practice.

Map before you speak, listen before you prescribe. This is the foundation of wisdom.

Move Toward the Good, not Toward the Crowd

> "The object of life is not to be on the side of the majority, but to escape finding oneself in the ranks of the insane."
>
> — Marcus Aurelius

Moving toward the good, not toward the crowd, isn't about rebellion or isolation. It's about alignment. It is about choosing the path that cultivates virtue, mastery, and clarity. This alignment is essential even when it's quiet, even when it's unpopular.

In life, we see a recurring pattern: People drift toward what's popular, what's loud, what's easy. They mimic trends, chase validation, and measure progress by applause, clicks, likes, or follows. We are all susceptible to this behavior.

The crowd becomes the compass. And the good, the true, the beautiful, the enduring, it is all left behind. Think of it this way, the crowd is no smarter than a monkey, sometimes clever, but never smart.

Why do we fall for this mimicking of trends? Why do we lean into what is popular and want to belong so badly that we compromise our integrity? From childhood, we're taught to fit in. We are socially conditioned to follow the group, to be liked. This instinct, once imperative for survival, now often dilutes our individuality.

Historically the threat of banishment was used to control the masses, assuring social order, and purifying the community. For example, in 1635 Roger Williams was banished from the Massachusetts Bay Colony for expressing views that threatened the power of the Puritan religious authorities who ran it. While he went on to found the colony of Rhode Island, he could just as easily have starved to death in the wilderness.

Even today, humans remain social animals. We fear being cut off from society. Algorithms reward conformity. We swim in echo chambers. Viral clips favor spectacle. The quiet discipline of daily practice rarely trends.

Sadly, we fear solitude. Standing up and walking toward the good often means walking alone. Alone can feel uncertain and attack the ego with second-guessing and rumination. Rather than being feared, this should be embraced. It is information to be used, not for acceptance but for auditing.

When we recognize this drift, it stings. We see how often we've worked for praise instead of progress. How often have we moved with the crowd instead of toward our calling? Seriously, think about it. The discernment hurts a little, doesn't it?

Never fear, this realization is a gift. It's the beginning of recalibration.

Think of Musashi Miyamoto, the legendary swordsman. He walked alone, carrying no banner but his own discipline. His writings do not teach popularity. Both *Go Rin No Sho* and *Dokkodo* teach precision, presence, and purpose.

The solution is not a dramatic one-and-done act. It's directional, we swerve from side-to-side and up and down. It's easy to drift. We must consistently and with effort add energy, keep reacquiring the target.

We solve this by choosing the good repeatedly. By asking ourselves, "Is this choice aligned with virtue, with mastery, with truth?" rather than asking, "Will this impress others?"

The good is magnetic. When we move toward it, we feel it. Our training deepens. Our mind clears. Our relationships strengthen. The crowd may not notice, but the soul does. And when the crowd does notice, it is often not good. Expect to be attacked as evil will notice you first. You are a threat to their idea or behavior.

Dr. Myles Munroe wrote, "The greatest tragedy in life is not death, but a life that never realized its full potential." History shows this. Think of Jigoro Kano, the founder of *judo*. He didn't chase popularity. He refined a system that honored safety, efficiency, and mutual welfare. Today, millions train in his art, not because he followed the crowd, but because he followed the good.

Kano set high expectations for himself and for his students. He purportedly expelled Mitsuyo Maeda from the *Kodokan* in 1904 for fighting for money. Maeda was one of the best, but it made no difference to Kano. Maeda's actions conflicted with Kano's strict code of ethics which led to them parting ways. Part of this code emphasized *judo* as a path of moral and physical education, not as a commercial spectacle. Kano demanded that all his disciples to follow the rules, regardless of skill or popularity.

To move toward the good is to move toward mastery, integrity, and peace. It's not loud. It's not crowded. But it's real.

Legacy is Fidelity in Quiet Hours

"To lead people, walk behind them."

— Lao Tzu

Legacy is shaped not in the spotlight, but in the shadow of daily fidelity to principle. Whether you're a teacher, a parent, or a work-a-day Joe, this is for anyone who has ever wondered, "How do I leave something behind that matters"?

We live in a time where legacy is often mistaken for visibility. Followers, accolades, viral moments. But the deeper question remains: What endures? Most legacies are unlabeled yet are passed on as an act or belief without the handle of attribution.

Many of the most enduring figures in martial arts, Morihei Ueshiba, Jigoro Kano, and Gichin Funakoshi, weren't chasing fame. They were refining principles, day after day.

Other examples are outside of the world of martial arts. For instance, Søren Kierkegaard was a Danish philosopher who often wrote under a pseudonym. He was about the idea, not the accolades, living a quiet life of bachelorhood and thought. Nevertheless, his work heavily influenced philosophers (e.g., Jean-Paul Sartre, Martin Heidegger, Ludwig Wittgenstein), writers (e.g., Franz Kafka and Henrik Ibsen), psychotherapists (e.g., Carl Rogers and Rollo May), artists like Edvard Munch, and filmmakers like Carl Theodor Dreyer long after his death in 1855.

The problem is subtle, we forget that legacy is shaped in mundane, hard work that has no flash for the public but carries internal reward. This drift from principle to performance has roots. We're conditioned to seek results quickly. Fidelity to principle is slow and often invisible. Medals and rankings become primary over internal alignment, which often is pushed to the back of the theater.

So, what happens when we lose our direction? We begin to feel hollow. Life becomes mechanical. Our relationships lose depth. We have all seen people with a form but no presence. They move well through life, but they don't move others. And we have seen the opposite, a quiet giant whose every gesture radiates integrity. No spotlight.

The solution isn't dramatic. It's daily.

Legacy is shaped through repetition with reverence. Through showing up, even when it's inconvenient. Through holding the line, not because it's easy, but because it's right.

Jigoro Kano once said, "The purpose of *judo* is to perfect oneself and contribute to society." He didn't say "win medals." He said, "perfect oneself." Win, lose, or draw, that's a daily act. Perfection is impossible, of course, yet striving for perfection sets our direction, our target. Our goal. As Vince Lombardi said, "Perfection is not attainable, but if we chase perfection we can catch excellence."

Because the principle is magnetic. When you live it, others feel it. Peers respect it. And over time, it shapes culture. Contrary to popular opinion, legacy isn't what you leave behind. It's what you live into others.

Legacy isn't built in the grand moments. It's shaped in the quiet ones. In the way you lace your shoes. In the way you greet your teacher. In the way you train when no one's watching.

Fidelity to principle is the forge. And every day is a chance to shape something that endures. So, wherever you are at your work, in the classroom, or in the silence of an early morning, remember that your legacy is already forming.

Shape it with care.

"Excellence is never an accident. It is always the result of high intention, sincere effort, and intelligent execution; it represents the wise choice of many alternatives. Choice, not chance, determines your destiny."

Aristotle

Conclusion

> "He who reigns within himself,
> and rules passions, desires, and
> fears, is more than a king."
>
> — John Milton

This book had been a guide to aligning your mind, body, and spirit so that you can live with clarity, purpose, and integrity. Drawing on wisdom from philosophy, martial arts, and historic figures, we have emphasized the importance of deliberate practices such as silence, disciplined training, intentional speech, strategic withdrawal, and structured systems to step into your sovereignty and reclaim control over your inner life.

We have challenged you to reject distractions, embrace solitude for refinement, and build a life that reflects your personal values while contributing meaningfully to the world. Through actionable insights and timeless principles, we hope that we have inspired you to govern your inner republic.

Now that you have the tools, we invite you to become the architect of your own clarity, purpose, and legacy. Begin each day with deliberate practices that align your thoughts, actions, and values. Embrace silence, refine your skills, and build systems that reflect your true self. Reject distractions, engage with challenges, and move toward the good, not the crowd.

Your inner republic awaits. Shape your life of authenticity, mastery, and meaningful impact. The time to act is now, step into your sovereignty and forge your destiny.

Profiles of Wisdom

We have referenced a variety of influential thinkers, leaders, and visionaries throughout this book. You may already know who they are, but if you do not or would like to learn a little more, here are their brief biographies:

- **Abraham Lincoln** (1809 – 1865) was the 16th president of the United States, best known for preserving the Union during the American Civil War and abolishing slavery through the Emancipation Proclamation and the 13th Amendment.

- **Annie Dillard** (1945 –) is an American author, best known for her Pulitzer Prize-winning book, *Pilgrim at Tinker Creek*. She is a prolific writer of essays, memoirs, and fiction, with themes often exploring the intersection of nature, spirituality, and philosophy. She taught at several colleges, including Wesleyan University, before becoming Professor Emerita.

- **Annie Duke** (1965 –) is an American former professional poker player. She is an author, speaker, and expert in decision science. Known as "The Duchess of Poker," she won the 2004 World Series of Poker Tournament of Champions. She earned over $4M in tournament winnings before retiring from the game, making her the sixth winningest female player of all time as of this writing.

- **Aristotle** (384 – 322 BC) is considered one of the most influential thinkers in Western history, making significant contributions to logic, science, and ethics. A Greek philosopher, he studied under Plato for 20 years before founding his own school, the Lyceum, and tutoring Alexander the Great.

- **Arthur Schopenhauer** (1788 – 1860) was a German philosopher. He was best known for his pessimism and his influential work, *The World as Will* and *Representation*. He proposed that human existence is driven by an irrational, insatiable metaphysical force he called "will." His work influenced later existentialists and psychologists, including Nietzsche, Freud, and Heidegger.

- **Ayn Rand** (1905 – 1982) was a Russian-American novelist, philosopher, and playwright best known for developing the philosophical system of Objectivism. She wrote the influential novels *The Fountainhead* and *Atlas Shrugged*. Rand was born in St. Petersburg, Russia. She witnessed the Bolshevik Revolution before emigrating to the United States in 1926.

- **Baruch Spinoza** (1632 – 1677) was a Dutch philosopher of Portuguese-Jewish descent. His radical ideas laid the groundwork for the Enlightenment and modern biblical criticism. His magnum opus, *Ethics*, presented a vision of God and nature as one unified substance.

- **Bill Watterson** (1958 –) is an American cartoonist, best known as the creator of the globally popular and acclaimed comic strip *Calvin and Hobbes*. He is known for his artistic integrity, refusal to license his characters, and his subsequent retreat from public life after ending his comic strip at the peak of its popularity in 1995. Since retiring he has become an accomplished painter and occasionally creates new artwork for charity.

- **Bishop Robert Barron** (1959 –) is a prominent American Catholic bishop, theologian, and evangelist, best known as the founder of Word on Fire Catholic Ministries.
- **Booker T. Washington** (1856 – 1915) was an African American educator, author, and political leader who advocated for economic advancement through vocational training and self-reliance. Born into slavery, he nevertheless became an advisor to U.S. presidents, including Theodore Roosevelt. He founded the Tuskegee Institute in 1881, built it into a well-respected organization, and remained its leader until he died.
- **C. S. Lewis** (1898 – 1963) was a British writer and scholar who was born in Belfast, studied at Oxford University, served in World War I, and became a professor at both Oxford and Cambridge. A former atheist, his conversion to Christianity profoundly influenced his writings. His best-known work is the fantasy series *The Chronicles of Narnia*.
- **Carl Jung** (1875 – 1961) was a Swiss psychiatrist who founded analytical psychology. He became the first president of the International Psychoanalytic Association and was initially seen as Freud's successor before they had a falling out. He is known for introducing concepts like the collective unconscious, archetypes, and introversion/extroversion, which formed the basis for the modern Myers-Briggs assessment and personality tool.
- **Chris Langan** (1952 –), often called, "The smartest man in America," is an independent thinker and horse rancher known for his exceptionally high IQ, reportedly somewhere between 195 and 210. He developed the Cognitive-Theoretic Model of the Universe, a philosophical framework aiming to unify science and theology.

- **Confucius** (551 – 479 BC) was a Chinese philosopher and political thinker whose ideas became the foundation of Confucianism. Born in the state of Lu during a time of social unrest, he emphasized moral integrity, filial piety, and the cultivation of virtuous leadership.

- **David Richo** (1940 –) is a psychotherapist, teacher, and author known for integrating Jungian, poetic, and mythic perspectives with Buddhist and Christian spiritual practices to help people with their psychological and spiritual growth and relationships. He focuses on topics like mindfulness, and dealing with one's "shadow self," as well as concepts such as the "Five A's of Love," which he defined as Attention, Acceptance, Appreciation, Affection, and Allowing.

- **Don Draper** is a fictional character portrayed by actor John Hamm, the enigmatic and charismatic protagonist of AMC's acclaimed series *Mad Men*, a 1960s-set drama exploring identity, ambition, and the American dream.

- **Dr. Myles Munroe** (1954 – 2014) was a Bahamian evangelical leader, author, and speaker. He founded the Bahamas Faith Ministries International. The author of 40 books, he was known for his teachings on leadership and purpose.

- **Edgar Ætheling** (1051 – 1126) was the last male heir of the Anglo-Saxon royal House of Wessex, briefly proclaimed King of England in 1066, but never crowned due to submitting to William the Conqueror. For a while Edgar then lived in exile, supported rebellions against William, but later served under William and his successors as Duke and Earl of Cambridge.

- **Elon Musk** (1971 –) is a South African-born entrepreneur known for co-founding companies like PayPal, SpaceX, Neuralink, and Tesla. He purchased the social media service Twitter, which he renamed X, in 2022. As of this writing, he is the richest man in the world.

- **Fedor Vladimirovich Emelianenko** (1976 –) is a retired Russian mixed martial artist widely regarded as one of the greatest heavyweight fighters in MMA history. He was nicknamed "The Last Emperor."

- **Francis Bacon** (1561 – 1626) was an English philosopher, scientist, lawyer, and statesman known for his role in the Scientific Revolution. He championed the scientific method, advocating for a new way of acquiring knowledge through empirical evidence and inductive reasoning rather than the old reliance on Aristotle.

- **Fyodor Dostoevsky** (1821 – 1881) was a Russian novelist known for his psychological depth and exploration of faith, suffering, and freedom. His most famous works included *Crime and Punishment*, *The Idiot*, and *The Brothers Karamazov*.

- **Gaius Cassius Longinus** (~ 86 BC – 42 BC) was a Roman senator, general, and the principal architect of the conspiracy to assassinate Julius Caesar, driven by a staunch belief in preserving the Roman Republic. He resented Caesar's growing power and persuaded Marcus Junius Brutus to join his plot. After the assassination, he was defeated by Caesar's allies at the Battle of Philippi and committed suicide.

- **George E. P. Box** (1919–2013) was a British-American statistician who made significant contributions to quality control, experimental design, and time-series analysis. After initially studying chemistry, World War II led him to teach himself statistics, analyze, and experiment with data. He co-founded the University of Wisconsin's statistics department.

- **George S. Patton** (1885 – 1945) was an American general, known for his aggressive tactics and blunt leadership during WWII. After serving in the first world war, he rose through the ranks to become a key commander in second, leading the invasion of Sicily, the breakout from Normandy, and playing a pivotal role in the Battle of the Bulge.

- **Gichin Funakoshi** (1868 – 1957) was a pioneering Okinawan martial artist who is widely regarded as the father of modern karate. He founded the Shotokan style.

- **Heraclitus** (~ 535 BC – 475 BC) was a pre-Socratic Greek philosopher who was born in Ephesus. He is known for his ideas about constant change and the unity of opposites, believing that the universe is in constant flux, famously writing, "You cannot step into the same river twice."

- **James Clear** (1986 –) is an author, speaker, and entrepreneur known for his work on habits, decision-making, and continuous improvement. Recovering from a severe injury profoundly influenced his focus on the power of small, consistent habits, a theme he built his career on and elucidated in his book *Atomic Habits*.

- **Jigoro Kano** (1860 – 1938) was a Japanese educator, reformer, and martial artist best known as the founder of *judo*. Beyond martial arts, Kano was a progressive thinker who promoted international exchange and served on the International Olympic Committee, helping pave the way for *judo*'s global recognition.

- **John Milton** (1608 – 1674) is considered the most significant English writer after William Shakespeare. He spent his final years in seclusion after losing his eyesight, relying on assistants to transcribe his most famous works, including the epic poem *Paradise Lost*, which was published in 1667.

- **John Stuart Mill** (1806 – 1873) was a British philosopher, economist, and political reformer known for his advocacy of liberty, individualism, and women's rights. His influential works included *On Liberty*, *Utilitarianism*, and *The Subjection of Women*.

- **Julian of Norwich** (~ 1342 – 1416) was an English mystic, theologian, and anchoress best known for her groundbreaking work *Revelations of Divine Love*, the earliest surviving book in English written by a woman.

- **Julius Caesar** (100 – 44 BC) was a Roman general, statesman, and author whose military conquests and political reforms transformed the Roman Republic and paved the way for the Roman Empire.

- **King Harold II** (unknown – 1066), also known as Harold Godwinson, was the last crowned Anglo-Saxon king of England, reigning briefly in 1066 before his death at the Battle of Hastings.

- **Lao Tzu** (~ 604 BC – unknown) was a Chinese philosopher, regarded as the founder of Taoism. He is also cited as the author of the *Tao Te Ching*, a foundational text of Eastern philosophy. He is believed to have lived during the 6th century BC. Lao Tzu emphasized living in harmony with the *Tao*, the natural, ineffable way of the universe.

- **Leo Tolstoy** (1828 – 1910) was a Russian writer and moral philosopher, best known for his epic novels *War and Peace* and *Anna Karenina*. His work often explored themes of morality, social injustice, and the human condition. His philosophy of nonviolent resistance influenced important figures like Mahatma Gandhi and Martin Luther King Jr.

- **Leopold I of Austria** (1640 – 1705), known as "The Glorious," was a Habsburg duke who ruled Austria and Styria from 1308 until his death in 1326, sharing power with his brother Frederick the Fair.

- **Lucius Annaeus Seneca** (~ 4 BC – 65 AD) was a Roman philosopher, statesman, dramatist, and orator, known for his essays, tragedies, and letters. A tutor to the emperor Nero, his life was shaped by political successes and setbacks, ultimately leading to Nero ordering him to suicide which he committed with composure. His pragmatic and practical philosophy, which explored how to live a good life amidst compromise and hardship, remains highly influential today.

- **Mahatma Gandhi** (1869 – 1948) was an Indian lawyer and political ethicist who used nonviolent resistance to lead his country to independence from British rule in 1947. He is known for his philosophy of *satyagraha*, or "truth force," which heavily influenced civil rights and freedom movements worldwide.

- **Marcus Antonius**, a.k.a. Mark Antony (83 – 30 BC) was a Roman general and politician, famed for his alliance with Julius Caesar and his romantic and political partnership with Cleopatra VII of Egypt.

- **Marcus Aurelius** (121 – 180) was a Roman emperor and Stoic philosopher. He is known for his masterwork, *Meditations*. He ruled from 161 to 180, guiding the empire through wars, plagues, and political unrest. As a Stoic, he believed in rational self-mastery, duty to the common good, and aligning one's actions with nature and reason.

- **Marcus Junius Brutus** (~ 85 – 42 BC) was a Roman politician and philosopher best known for his leading role in the assassination of Julius Caesar, driven by a belief in preserving the Roman Republic.

- **Marcus Licinius Crassus** (115 – 53 BC) was a Roman general and statesman known for his immense fortune, political alliance with Caesar and Pompey in the First Triumvirate, and his role in the defeat of Spartacus's slave revolt. Afterward he invaded Parthia seeking military glory to rival Pompey's, was lured into a trap, and murdered during a truce that followed his defeat at the Battle of Carrhae.

- **Mike Mentzer** (1951 – 2001) was a groundbreaking American bodybuilder, author, and philosopher. He is best known for his "Heavy Duty" training system and his intellectual approach to fitness. Mentzer won titles like Mr. America in 1976 and the heavyweight division of Mr. Olympia in 1979.

- **Mitsuyo Maeda** (1878 – 1941), also known as Count Combat or Conde Koma, was a Japanese *judoka* and prizefighter whose global travels and teachings laid the foundation for Brazilian *Jiu-Jitsu* when he settled in Brazil and taught *judo* to Gastão Gracie.

- **Miyamoto Musashi** (1584 – 1645) was a legendary Japanese swordsman, strategist, and philosopher. Often called "*Kensei*," the sword-saint of Japan, Musashi is best known for his skill in dueling along with his influential treatise *Go Rin No Sho*, *The Book of Five Rings*. Musashi fought in over 60 duels, never losing one, and developed a distinctive two-sword technique he called *Niten Ichi-Ryū*.

- **Morihei Ueshiba** (1883 – 1969) was a Japanese martial artist and spiritual thinker best known as the founder of *Aikido*, a modern martial art that blends physical technique with philosophical and ethical principles.

- **Norm Macdonald** (1959 – 2021) was a Canadian comedian, writer, and actor celebrated for his dry wit, philosophical humor, and distinctive delivery. Macdonald was revered by peers for his originality and subversive intelligence.

- **Octavian**, later known as Augustus (63 BC – 14 AD), was the founder and first emperor of the Roman Empire, ruling from 27 BC until his death and ushering in the *Pax Romana*, a period of relative peace and stability across the empire.

- **Padre Pio** (1887 – 1968), born Francesco Forgione in southern Italy, was a Capuchin friar, mystic, and Catholic priest. He was renowned for his spirituality, healings, and the stigmata which he reportedly bore for most of his life. He was canonized a saint by Pope John Paul II in 2002.

- **Plato** (~ 428 – 347 BC) was a foundational Greek philosopher whose ideas shaped the course of Western thought. A student of Socrates and teacher of Aristotle, Plato founded the Academy in Athens. The Academy was the first institution of higher learning in the Western world.

- **Ralph Waldo Emerson** (1803 – 1882) was an American essayist, poet, and philosopher who led the Transcendentalist movement in the mid-19th century. He became a Unitarian minister but resigned after his wife's death to pursue a career as a lecturer and writer. His philosophy, which emphasized individualism, self-trust, and a connection between humanity and nature, made him a central figure in American literature.

- **Ram Dass** (1931 – 2025) was born Richard Alpert. He was an American psychologist, spiritual teacher, and the author of the book *Be Here Now*, known for popularizing Eastern spirituality and *yoga* in the West. After a career in academia that included researching psychedelics at Harvard University, he traveled to India, where his *guru* gave him the name Ram Dass which means, "Servant of God."

- **René Descartes** (1596 – 1650) was a French philosopher, mathematician, and scientist. He is widely regarded as the father of modern Western philosophy. He pioneered a method of systematic doubt to arrive at foundational truths, famously declaring *"Cogito, ergo sum"* which translates as, "I think, therefore I am."

- **Roger Williams** (1603 – 1683) was an English Puritan minister who founded the colony of Providence (later known as Rhode Island). Banished from the Massachusetts Bay Colony for his radical views championing individual liberty, he purchased land from the native Americans, making his new colony a refuge for those seeking freedom of conscience.

- **Søren Kierkegaard** (1813 – 1855) was a Danish philosopher, theologian, and writer considered a precursor to existentialism. His work explored the individual's existence, faith, and the nature of truth, often using pseudonyms to present complex philosophical dilemmas that encouraged personal responsibility for one's beliefs and choices.

- **St. Anthony of the Desert** (251 – 356) is revered as the father of Christian monasticism. Born in Egypt in 251 to a wealthy family, after the death of his parents he gave away his inheritance and retreated into the desert to live a life of solitude, prayer, and spiritual warfare.

- **St. Benedict of Nursia** (~ 480 – 547) was an Italian monk and the founder of Western Christian monasticism, best known for composing the Rule of St. Benedict, a guide for communal monastic life that shaped religious practice for centuries.

- **Stephen R. Covey** (1932 – 2012) was an American educator, author, business, and leadership guru, most famous for his book *The 7 Habits of Highly Effective People*. After earning degrees from the University of Utah, Harvard Business School, and Brigham Young University, he founded the Covey Leadership Center whose mission is, "To develop principle-centered leaders of character and competence, who elevate society." Co-author Lawrence Kane is a graduate.

- **Sun Tzu** (544 – 496 BC) is an honorific that means "Master Sun." According to historians, his given name was Wu. King Ho-Lu, with Sun Tzu at his side, defeated the powerful Ch'u state in 506 BC, capturing their capital city of Ying. He then headed north and subdued the states of Qi and Chin to forge his empire. Sun Tzu recorded his winning strategies in a book titled *Art of War* sometime around 510 BC. It is the earliest surviving and most revered tome of its kind.

- **The Desert Fathers** were early Christian monks and hermits who lived primarily in the Wadi El Natrun, which was known as Skete in their day. They withdrew into the Egyptian wilderness during the 3rd and 4th centuries. Their goal was to pursue lives of radical simplicity, prayer, and spiritual discipline.

- **Thomas Crum** (1992 –) is an author and presenter in the fields of conflict resolution, peak performance, and stress management. He developed the "The Thomas Crum Approach," designed to help people become more centered under conflict, more resourceful when facing challenges, and more effective under stress.

- **Tony Hsieh** (1947 – 2020) was an American entrepreneur and venture capitalist best known as the CEO of the online shoe retailer Zappos, which he sold to Amazon for over $1B in 2009. He was known for cultivating a company culture that focused on employee happiness and customer service, which he detailed in his book Delivering Happiness.

- **Tony Robbins** (1960 –) is a globally renowned motivational speaker, author, and life strategist whose work has empowered millions to transform their lives through personal development and peak performance leveraging neuro-linguistic programming and firewalking. He is known for his high-energy seminars as well for coaching celebrities and business leaders.

- **Ulysses S. Grant** (1822 – 1885) graduated from West point, served with distinction in the Mexican-American war, but struggled in civilian life. After the American Civil War began, he reentered military service, rose through the ranks, and led the Union Army to victory. He was elected the 18th president of the United States.

- **Vince Lombardi** (1889 – 1971) was an American football coach, known for leading the Green Bay Packers to victory in five NFL championships between 1961 and 1967, along with winning Super Bowls I and II. His demanding and disciplined coaching style, emphasis on fundamentals, and leadership philosophy made him one of the most influential figures in sports history. The Super Bowl trophy is named in his honor.

- **William James** (1842 – 1910) was an American philosopher and psychologist who co-founded the school of pragmatism. He established the first psychology lab at Harvard University and championed a philosophy that emphasizes the practical consequences of ideas. His book, *The Principles of Psychology*, was a pioneering work at the time.

- **William Shakespeare** (1564 – 1616) was an English playwright, poet, and actor widely regarded as the greatest writer in the English language. Born in Stratford-upon-Avon, he authored 39 plays, 154 sonnets, and numerous poems. His writings explore the timeless themes of love, power, betrayal, and identity.

- **William the Conqueror** (1028 – 1087), also known as William I of England, was the Duke of Normandy who led the Norman invasion of England and won the pivotal Battle of Hastings in 1066, becoming the first Norman king of England.

About the Authors

Kris Wilder

Kris was inducted into the U.S. Martial Arts Hall of Fame in 2018. He runs the *Cheney Karate Academy*, a frequent destination for practitioners from around the world which also serves the local community. He has earned black belt rankings in three styles, karate, judo, and taekwondo, and often travels to conduct seminars across the United States, Canada, and Europe. His book, *The Way of Sanchin Kata*, was translated into Japanese, a rare honor for a Western karate practitioner.

A Nationally Board-Certified Life Coach and prolific author, Kris has lectured at Washington State University and Susquehanna University and served as an advisor for the Eastern Washington University Karate Club.

He spent about 15 years in the political and public affairs arena, working for campaigns from the local to national level. During this consulting career, he was periodically on staff for elected officials. His work also involved lobbying and corporate affairs. And, he was also a member of The Order of St. Francis (OSF), one of many active Apostolic Christian Orders.

Kris is the bestselling author of 34 books, including a Beverly Hills Book Award and Presidential Prize winner, a Living Now Book Award winner, a USA Best Book Awards winner, a National Indie Excellence Awards winner, three Independent Press Award winners, a Next Generation Indie Book Awards winner, and two Eric Hoffer award nominees. He has been interviewed on CNN, FOX, The Huffington Post, Thrillist, Nickelodeon, Howard Stern, and more.

Kris lives in Cheney, Washington. You can contact him through social media at: https://linktr.ee/KrisWilder.

Lawrence A. Kane

Lawrence was inducted into the American Martial Arts Alliance Hall of Honors in 2025. He is Head of Procurement at a leading diversified financial services company in the United States. He was inducted into the SIG Sourcing Supernova Hall of Fame in 2018 for visionary leadership in strategic sourcing, procurement, supplier innovation, and digital transformation. In 2023 he earned an EPIC Award for lifetime achievements in indirect procurement from ProcureCon.

Over the course of his career, he institutionalized world-class practices that earned the prestigious Global Excellence in Outsourcing award from IAOP and seven Future of Sourcing innovation awards from SIG, among other honors. He regularly advances thought leadership as a keynote speaker at industry conferences.

Lawrence has been studying and teaching martial arts since 1970, including a wide variety of traditional Asian styles, medieval swordsmanship, modern combatives, and close-quarters combat. The bestselling author of 31 books, he has been a guest on nationally syndicated and local radio shows (e.g., The Jim Bohannon Show, Biz Talk Radio), television programs (e.g., Fox Morning News), and podcasts (e.g., Art of Procurement, Negotiations Ninja Podcast, Sourcing Industry Landscape), and has also been interviewed by reporters from *Information Week*, *Le Matin*, *CPO Strategy*, *Forbes*, *Jissen*, and *Computerworld*, among other publications.

Lawrence lives in Seattle, Washington. You can contact him directly at lakane@ix.netcom.com or connect on LinkedIn (www.linkedin.com/in/lawrenceakane).

Explore More Books from The Authors:

Kris Wilder and Lawrence Kane are the bestselling, award-winning authors of *Musashi's Dokkodo*, *The Little Black Book of Violence*, *10 Rules of Karate, Dude, The World's Gonna Punch You in the Face*, and *Martial Arts and Your Life*, among numerous other titles. Discover more below…

Kris Wilder

Lawrence A. Kane

www.ingramcontent.com/pod-product-compliance
Lightning Source LLC
LaVergne TN
LVHW051841080426
835512LV00018B/3013